Notes from Other Worlds

Susan Gray

Published by Playdead Press 2014

© Susan Gray 2014

Susan Gray has asserted her rights under the Copyright, Design and Patents Act, 1988, to be identified as the author of this work.

A CIP catalogue record for this book is available from the British Library.

ISBN 978-1-910067-19-2

Caution
All rights whatsoever in the text are strictly reserved and application for performance should be sought through the author before rehearsals begin. No performance may be given unless a license has been obtained.

This book is sold subject to the condition that it shall not by way of trade or otherwise, be lent, resold, hired out, or otherwise circulated without the publisher's prior consent in any form of binding or cover other than that in which it is published and without a similar condition including this condition being imposed on the subsequent purchaser.

Printed by BPUK

Playdead Press
www.playdeadpress.com

Acknowledgements

There are many people that I'd like to thank, for different reasons. Apologies in advance if I've missed anyone out. I'd like to start first with my parents, who could've easily disapproved of my artistic career trajectory, but have instead supported me in every way conceivable. Likewise to my family - I know especially how much my Grandma and Nan have been anticipating my first book - I hope it lives up to their expectations! For those who are no longer here - including my Grandpa and my Uncle Mike, both of whom supported me so much - I also thank them. Much love to them.

I'd also like to thank the Roundhouse and the Poetry Collective for giving me the courage to perform spoken word, which led onto the theatre writing and monologues. I'd also like to thank Denis Vaughan who gave me that opportunity to edit Enigma, the creative writing magazine after graduating and knowing that creativity still beckoned after university. Thank you to the lecturers at Brunel (especially Max Kinnings and David Fulton) for fostering a love for the creative and dramatic word. I'd also like to thank Adam Roberts for all his support during my PhD in general.

Thank you also to all my friends, especially Jorge Ba-Oh for all his support from day one. If I listed you all, it could be a book of its own. Maybe I'll write that separately. Love to you all and to Playdead Press.

Contents

1.	Introduction	5
2.	3 Degrees	9
3.	The Other Roof	19
4.	Muscle Memory	24
5.	Eight	32
6.	A Russian Doll Case	35
7.	Mercurial Harbour	44
8.	Not me/Not I	52
9.	Crowdfund The Topia	56
10.	Object Meets Subject	60
11.	The Happiness Architect	77
12.	Oblique	81

Introduction

Science Fiction is a genre known for its ever shifting guise. From what was known as a literature of ideas – the extrapolations into an exciting and yet terrifying future to the dwellings of dystopia, warnings to those who continue to live such reckless lifestyles as well as those who believed that the iron fist would be in vogue and they'd be first in line to try on the gloves.

It is arguably now a visual culture – HD and 3D explosions, the chalk-like trails left from a spaceship using an interstellar warp drive, FTL being the equivalent of 5th gear on a car (although that's often been the case in Science Fiction). Now it is a multiplicity of different forms, recently adopted by the academic crowd. What was a genre left on the sidelines has now sprung into mainstream culture. Comic cons, videogames, cosplay and anime are now for the "cool kids" as well as the "nerds" who hid themselves away in their room, devouring this culture – it's the worst kept secret.

What I want to home in on with these Science Fiction monologues is the *character* - but not just that. There's a tricky balancing act as far as the form goes - I want to be able to create the pressure of the SF tropes acting on these characters, which brings out their relationship to the world and vice versa. These are think pieces, yes, but through a particular filter of being.

One can be hard pressed to pick a specific character they'd like to be, and it's possibly unlikely that it's because of their personality or their back story. It's the stuff that the character gets to *do*. Everything is carefully orchestrated and the character is just the stave upon which the notes, the plot points, are placed.

In *Notes From Other Worlds*, the characters take the stage and spotlight. Their circumstances are unseen but narrated. They're not the omniscient narrators that we can be accustomed to. We don't have the pleasure of multiple viewpoints to one action so that we get a rounded view. They don't know all the answers. We have to fill them in – and so everyone can take part in these stories.

But what differentiates these SF monologues from SF short stories is that I would love to see them performed. Not just read, or even read aloud. Performed, directed, and putting the actor's own stance and interpretation into them. Because of this, the stage direction is minimal - there is a paragraph explaining the backdrop so there are some crib notes for the performer to work with. These have been written with no gender in mind. Any reference to age is for a specific reason.

The book revolves around different SF tropes – ones that we would immediately think of when we see those two letters put together in that way. The monologues involved include time travel, technological novums, an interstellar journey, a robot story, a virtual reality story, dystopian/utopian perspectives and more. I won't spell these out for you as there are many that straddle these – but the importance is on their reaction. The focus is on how people would live with these ideas – a moment of alterity through which we can see humanity in a different way (hopefully). After all, isn't that what the dramatic voice aims to do? Why we talk and most importantly, why we listen?

In Science Fiction Theatre, we don't have the fancy devices and visual detail that the TV and the Cinema have (increasingly) in spades. We have to show you something more than words as opposed to the novel, and we're to fill in the gaps by our presentation. Of reaction. Of being overwhelmed or overcoming these SF tropes.

We have these monologues as case studies, as ends in themselves as well as each piece being connected, like candy beads on a string. These stories are actually depicting different angles of experience on one planet, one that is heading towards a certain fate. You can try and figure it out, if you like. Tweet me @Suzie_Gee for your different responses. These range in length - for short, medium and longer pieces. There is also a monologue that can work as a duologue or one where half is recorded - more of a monodrama.

If you do choose to perform these (and I hope you do), play around with the characters, get inside their heads. I'd be very interested to see what you come up with. I'm having a noodle around myself – you may see some readings and Youtube recordings by myself.

What, I hear you say? The writer is noodling around with these characters? Yes – I'm afraid I don't have all the answers either. That's always the best way, though.

3 Degrees

The character is seated - in a booth - the recipient is unseen. They are part of a rehabilitation program, which involves personal therapy and intermittent opportunities to engage in mindfulness. They should address the audience as though the person is there.

You know, it's great to talk to you. Just you. I've turned the I-nfo off — well, at least her volume is down so it's bearable. It doesn't feel like my brain is struggling to grow, a tree from the seed that strangles and sap the energy of the conversation altogether — it's a quiet, subtle, hum.

It's been a while since I've done this. Please bear with me. It's hard, like shadow boxing and hoping my air — the subtle changes in frequency - will hit the right person. I'm just flailing, hoping to connect. It's so... vulgar. Would you agree? No. No. After all, you're still listening to me, right? That's what this place is for, after all.

It's quiet though, isn't it? It's a tough crowd. You know, silence and that.

My... the I-nfo told me that people used to be astonished at the noise of industry — the common soundscape in those days

— towering skyscrapers inducing awe, the circulatory system of workers with the colours blending like plasma in the blood stream, the excitable heat, the spit and hiss of the smoke snakes. They inhaled it and felt it assimilating back into them, the pulses of agency and dynamics that start the cycle again... I think I came up with the imagery. It's hard to remember, but that's not important right now. She (I call it a she, I don't know why) just told me about how it was in those days. I just plonked the pieces together with senses that I'm used to, memories that hold similar association — she said I was good with that, but to keep it to a minimum. She suggested a certain number of metaphors, a certain number of similes. Associations kept to 3 degrees, maximum. Oh, I didn't mean to tell you that. Now you'll be listening out for that. Forget I said that. I don't want to distract you any more than I should. Distraction leads to temptation that leads to annihilation.

It makes sense. It makes sense.

For example, I might not hear her warning me about an imminent crash with the outside world. When we used to build empires, I mean they, everything was a projection. Buildings sprung as an extension of our inner system, begging to be noticed under that thin veil of cloud, to draw us upwards to notice the world that existed there – for those inside to feel superior, looking out upon their own concrete creations. From what she told me, there used to be pyramids, beautiful structures that felt cold and hard under the fingertips – the rusty smell that told you a story of its own. But it's not always the right tale, is it? A kid could think that it was a candy store, or a place where you buy souvenirs if he didn't have his own tech. He could be petrified, afraid of the compact spaces. Ignorance is a bitch, huh? Now, now... everything is smaller – folded, intimate, compacted, existing within us. Sometimes I don't know if it's pride or... you know... shame.

Did you hear that?

It can't be shame. Silly me. It makes things easier. It makes sense. Everyone can use their own special system. We all know each other, it's a partnership. Otherwise we may as well be those towers, those pyramids; a cover, a barricade. You need to know a certain pass key – they called it hieroglyphics – to understand it. It's an artefact, an old form of augmented reality. People used to love mystery, to sit around and ponder something they didn't truly understand. I can see its appeal to an extent, but then I get distracted. Do you? It's like they wish themselves ignorant so that they can keep on thinking. It's strange. Arthur C Clarke, he used to be one of those artistes, he called it failure of nerve or failure of imagination. He used to ponder all sorts about the future, as I recall. Maybe we've cracked the big puzzles now – the things we don't know are the things we don't need to know about. It's much better now. People loved mystery, this sort of mental masturbation. I tend to do it in private, of course – it's a sort of guilty pleasure, below the surface of what we know, right?

Yet here I am, talking to you – like I'm showing my neurosis off. I hope I haven't offended you. It's like I want something from you – social intercourse to the letter. Am I looking for truth when I'm talking to you, or do I want distraction? Something that the I-nfo tech can't... no, she knows everything... but she doesn't know ignorance, I guess. If I told her to tell me the wrong information, she could. But I'd have to prompt that from her. She can't lie. Sometimes I don't know where she ends and I begin. Does she rely on my words, or do I rely on her replies?

People did that – depended on each other for information. Can I ask you a direct representation of the temporal state from this side of the earth?

I'm laughing. How on earth did people ask each other for the time in an accurate measure? That's ridiculous. How would you structure the question, pinpoint something that doesn't stay still? I was being vague, of course. We see time trickling, dynamic – not static. How can you trust pinpointing the right kind of stranger? Taking people on at face value – it's worrying. Imagine any journey on that Autobus. Look at every passenger. They might be your long lost relative, just as adrift as you are, or in fact the last face you see before the life slips away out of your cold, grasping hands. Your soul mate (whatever that truly means) might be the one who barges past you and swears under their breath in your ear. The excuse was mystery. There's always an excuse.

My mouth is getting tired. I know we're supposed to have this exercise time, but it's so temperamental to get my jaws moving for this amount of time. How did people use to do it? They used to talk doing anything. Waiting in a queue, on the street – and yet they still had social conventions like this as if talking to people casually in an open environment wasn't enough. And the questions they used to ask – they smacked of ignorance and stupidity and vagueness and of ordinary. How is your day? How are you? They couldn't answer properly, so there were these sorts of conventions of conversation. You need to know the right words to keep things in stasis, in flow. I don't quite understand. Why should I create further mystery as a result? I'm fine – what did that even mean?

I know I'm blabbing, but my I-nfo tech gets tired of me thinking about this. I can anticipate her words, even though they're this low level hiss in my ear. Too many degrees of separation! You have taken too long on this detour. When I turn her on again, I'll apologise. When they patch in the new timetable, she'll understand – the government wants us to exercise our mouths again, to make us aware as a social unit. I'm sure you know by yours too. Chatting the breeze, they called it, recycled air - a way for us to let steam off. Just like those snakes, except that they're confined to in here.

I start a new job tomorrow. Did you know that? Oh, of course you didn't. You've turned it off too, haven't you? I could be lying. How about that? I might even be working for you, or you for me. I might even be your new boss in your fancy department – they'll be sending you the forms shortly. It's mad. Scary. How do I know that you're "you", if you get me? Sure, I can see certain things about you – your face and your eyes, your hair and so on. I can't see your status or title or what you've done. I can't see your CV or what you like doing. I don't know if we're related. I don't know if you've ever slept with anyone of my previous partners or even why you've been chosen to sit with me. Fiction always had to have a reason. Destiny dealt a hand at all times, reassured us that we were chosen; that these distractions meant something. It just feels empty if I think about it too much. We're pyramids, on this bench, in this voice gym, in this booth. I don't know if I've told you too much, or too little.

I don't have to walk far to get here, you know. Walking. I could've taken the Autobus but there's a pleasure in the activity — it's like a museum tour. I'm old fashioned, I guess. Do you walk yourself? I bet you do. You should be careful, because people can take advantage of it, you know. You're listening to your I-nfo and you're at one with yourself. Burrowed inside your own shell — your mind is. Your body's forgotten, neglected, in the cold — well, she stopped them. Stopped them, you ask? Yes, they came at me, wanted to attack me, that group. They stage old fashioned crimes, fists and that. I heard the whistle, the violence on the screaming air, suddenly taken prisoner. The pain was exhilarating; I have to admit, oh, the streaming! Adrenaline, that old drug!

She disabled them and allowed me to get through – you know, that gentle sharp shock. I never dialled it too high, you see. His nail caught on me and it felt like a breeze ripping through a sail - a gust of cold air to bring me to a new sense of awakening – a terrifying but thrilling experience. It was nothing really, but oh, the reprimanding!

If they were using their tech, you'd be dead. I wouldn't be living up to my side of the bargain. That's worse than annihilation for me. You know that.

I didn't think so. Maybe they're reliving the old life, the rough as well as the smooth. She knows more than me, so here I am. I can't complain.

Sentenced with a dose of mindfulness and the 3 degree rule.

It's an odd kind of action. Mindfulness – the act of cutting degrees like they used to do with weight. To cut off distractions, I guess, is to feel, to live. The program wanted for us to do this now – but they haven't told us when, how long for. Just an end time, that's all. I want to ask you, I do. Why are you here?

Right, if I'm your boss, I command you. Close your eyes for me. Thank you for your time and co-operation.

Right, I'm ready. Following the instructions. Over there.

I'm standing, I'm standing, my feet are planted against the concrete, toes are making full contact concrete; one species contacting another. I can feel my spine balance gently, accumulating, straining, sighing – sloshing with fluid. It feels odd; it feels like I'm turning into a machine. Do I want to feel fear? Do I want to prove them right? That what they do, what they have given us is correct? Being grateful, it's all about being grateful, right? I'm not sure if I like this – every man is an island, every man is an island. Do you feel that too? Everything's turning over, imploding in on itself. My hands are waving at gravity and my eyes are scrunching at the mere magnitude of it. No numbers, just affectation. Just feeling – it's like a brute atavistic power.

I want to turn it on again. I don't know. I'm torn. Time is up soon, anyway, I can feel it. Best to turn it on, best to bring us back into reality. Are you feeling OK? I can't tell. It's disorientating – like I'm floating in a vacuum. A new sort of blindness. I can't see beyond the surface and it frightens me. Maybe that's why these times are scheduled – to know what we've missed, to know just how lucky we are. Her voice lulls me into you know... a will... a mantra to continue, maybe... it was good to talk to you. I miss her. It was good talking to you, though, and I genuinely mean that. You made me realise what I'd lose if I didn't have her. I lost count on the degrees — I gorged myself on them. She'll forgive me once the timetable is patched. I'm sorry, Miss. I'm sorry.

The Other Roof

The character is fighting with their neighbour about the extravagance of the rich amongst the poor. People who are rich enough can buy life enhancements - and are seemingly squandering their newly found power amongst those that age. It's a newly bought jouissance, and the neighbour's ambition is to at least leave a lasting message of some value.

Do you really have to do this?

Jumping off that roof again?

You know I'm here. Obviously. You know, that... weird vision - some upgrade or other, with numbers that you can only imagine in them crazy futuristic books. Change yer height day by day. Just to keep stuff interesting. As if life isn't a challenge enough. Try having something to really suffer for. Not whether you outgrow your bloody clothes of something.

New eyes, tick. New bones, tick. Brain cells like a damn fancy hat.

You think I'm bitter? No, of course not. I love being the animal on display amongst the rich, extravagant humans.

Tiptoe over the boundary and you see real living. The music changes. Something clicks in the head and that.

I can't move. I can't afford to move everything, yes, but… Yes, it'd be best for everyone but…

Yes, it's your house, but…

Yes, they're bloody "invulnerable". What do you want me to call them? Angels? That's an old stereotype for calling kids, ain't it? Look, but just…

What I'm trying to say is… what's that word, tip of your tongue. Yeah. Consideration. Please be considerate towards your neighbours. I mean, how do you know that my husband or my wife didn't jump off a roof to end their own lives, huh? You might be taking the piss, mightn't you?

Oh, and what is this roof jumping about, anyway? Teaching them the values of life? Doesn't go down the drain when you can stuff money down it?

What if they try and stab someone, just for fun? Like those damn videogames those kids used to have? What if they stab someone who doesn't have that amount of tech? You really want to take that risk?

[beat]

I've heard about it, you know. It's in the head. We weren't meant to be made like this. You know that boy? They cut at his arms, his legs. Screwed up his mind properly, you know, couldn't leave the house for days - couldn't look at himself in the mirror. It wouldn't hurt him, you know, like physically - they knew that. But the mind can't handle it - it's the fear of being exposed like that. To see people who think they can have a crack at you. And your little brood snapping bones on the street. Unharmed. Not the best bloody sign to all and sundry, is it?

[beat]

You know what you could do with your kids? Set them the hardest conundrums of the age. Yeah, conundrums. Puzzles that take them a lifetime to sort out, they'll have enough of that. World peace, yeah, that's a good one. Peace builds bridges and War breaks em down again. That'd keep them occupied. At least be on the building side. Takes more brain power. Feels better too, probably.

Don't need to solve those health problems, lucky... kids.

[beat]

Am I making you feel guilty?

No, I haven't lost anyone by jumping off a roof! Don't be thick!

[beat]

Privilege has downsides too, I think. I'm not trying to rub some guilt on yer. Sure I won't be here in 50 years time when your kids would have upgraded to yanking body parts off of each other for laughs. But just think.

[beat]

No, that was a joke. A shit one, but you know. Making light.

[beat]

Look, take my little one. She'll be here still when I'm gone, touch wood.

You want her to go into a world where she feels afraid, unsafe? She doesn't have the power that you have, but she'll do the best with what she has. If she has any sense left in that big head of hers.

[beat]

Not going to lie - well, I don't know what truth snooping app you have, but I'm jealous. Fucking jealous. You know that? We were the first generation to get this... well you did, and I got to watch you stay the same. Learning, getting wiser by the quickening minute while I'm on a frigging time lapse. Look at me. We were the same bloody age.

But enough about me. This is about more than just me. Our mothers and fathers were the last to know about it. They knew it could be for us, right? And what? You think it's right to just jump off roofs, do all this self-destructive stuff, show off your wares because they fought for the right for it?

Oh come on, I can be all high and mighty too. Not reserved for you folk.

What I'm saying is —

Don't let it go to waste.

Muscle Memory

The character has "revived" the unknown recipient through a backed up virtual copy, which has been verified through contract and so on. However, the person who has signed it was from a past relationship. The anxiety and awkwardness are clearly evident as both characters do not know how to react.

It's not a one way street, you know.

The whole process. The reason you're here. No, no, I'm not trying to guilt trip you. Sheesh. No.

The thing is... well, the thing. Your bed's set up. Well, it's our bed you used to sleep in, right, but I don't want you to get the wrong idea. I don't know if you're tired, even. You know, when you have relatives round, you set their dinner up for them, get their bed made, ask them about their journey, whether it's been alright. The traffic and that. What the weather was like. But I'm not an idiot. That's the only kinda... protocol I've got stored up in here.

I mean, you've slept for a long time. I'm sure you want to have a walk around, get used to it all?

Ah... is that insensitive of me?

Maybe if I stop asking questions. Get you used to the place.

[Stands up, eagerly]

I can do a tour if you like.

No, that sounds wrong. A tour of a place you've always lived in? What a damn joke.

Right. I'm going to be straight with you because I think that's the least you deserve. You signed the contract and so did I, all that stuff. I can't patronise you, or more accurately, I shouldn't. You know these things.

[Paces towards the audience, bewildered]

You've been... not asleep, you're not 5 years old. Well, you're... you're... one week old in your take two? Not even that yet. You were at least 30 years old when you were... you know. I mean, you're alive now, so I can tell you that you were killed. Not even killed. Out of the game?

You used to be so insecure about your age – and you don't look a day over 30!

And here's me. Decrepit. Probably. All looks the same to me. Well, you probably look the same to you.

Yet you're here. That's the most important part. I mean, you don't look exactly how I remember you. You're still beautiful, of course! They say that in films, that's what everyone does. Everything goes on and on because that's how everyone would like it. That friends can meet up after years and everything's the same. Just a front, is all. You revert back to type but you're not the same, are you?

I know I'm going to sound patronising, so stop me if you've heard too little, like that's possible, or too much. Just so that we're on the same page.

OK. You wanted to be stored into the electronic ether and I've brought you back. Like you said. Like you signed. Before the accident... this was you and it's you now. So... don't think you have any ties to me whatsoever. I brought you back, yes, but that's it. I don't own you. You don't own me. We can be a partnership again, if that's what you want.

You don't even have to ask me what I've been doing since you've gone. It must be all kinds of shit to imagine what you might've missed out on. See, I said might! I could've been twiddling my thumbs for all you know. Cracking one out now and then over our last memories together.

Shit. Cracking one out. Where are my damn manners!

Ah, I wonder what you remember?

Muscle memory. You know, stuff you just "remember" doing. Nah that's not right. You know, when your muscles do the things you did before.

I'm doing the same. Recognising... people. People that you haven't seen for a while. Or come to accept that you haven't.

Without bringing it up. Just like when you call an old friend and nothing's changed and you can just pick up conversation... just without the things being the same. You can pick up a thread but it's been woven pretty tightly. Or something. That's one thing that the movies were right about.

Moving things with pictures.

Sorry, being facetious...

I've... got you some water! Yes! Do you feel thirsty, hungry?

[The character gestures behind them before walking off. Turns back. Stops]

[beat]

Oh, well. I'll leave it there then, just in case you need it...

So the thing is, I knew that this might be our actual goodbye. I mean, how ironic is that? When you're re-uploaded, you might not want a thing to do with me. No, it wasn't my fault. But what I'm saying is, would you give it another go with me?

Damn, you know, the sex was... good. How can I say the word sex and not how it was, how it felt, how it meant to me – damn modern ways of thinking. Sweaty mornings where we'd roll out of bed and go about our day the way nature intended. I sound like a bloody pervert now, don't I? If you didn't know all that happened.

I can give you a balanced potted history if you want.

Y'know, give you some crap memories and some good memories and you can weigh them up or drop them in a hat and pick them out and... damn, that's old fashioned. We can use the randomiser, story snippets of our life. I've collected them... to a point. I've hidden some, made some private - well, we all know how private those are, anyway.

I've lost sleep just knowing the damn things are there. That's when I preferred just having the mind to back these up. Not all these pockets of nightmares. No symbolism. Just the real damn thing. Ghosts, aren't they?

I'm sorry.

[beat]

You need time? Time's one thing we can do. I guess. More than anything.

It's a good thing to have.

[beat]

Ah... that chair? Really?

We sang songs in that chair. When we were going to be "big". Those bands, like groups of people making music, before it was made like sausages in a factory. Well, that's a lie. It's just that... I dunno... the meat tasted better then and...

No.

[beat]

This isn't going to be easy. I'm so fucking sorry. It can't be the same. It won't. It can't be like leaving a place because...

well, your mind probably stopped caring. The closure. That was it. I don't know what it blocked out. What it kept.

I'll pay for a hotel. All that stuff. I can open your bank account and get all your stuff back. There's the whole system for it and...

You're not the only one. There are people like you... oh, fuck. Came out wrong.

You can have a new name, new identity, anything you want. You can be the old you... but that seems harder, I guess. Legacies and all that stuff.

You'll be there and I'll be here. Same as ever.

Contact me if you want. If you want to know what happened. It can't be that accurate, of course. Humans, you know how it is. Oh for fuck's sake! I know you're human. Just... right.

Here's your wallet. Filled with all the chips and tricks. Call it a welcome gift from me. You can toss it later if you want. Just something to get you off the ground.

I'm not going to say that I loved you and I still love you. That'd be pointless, right? It's not like your mind just says that.

Right. I wish you luck on all your future endeavours... like a fucking failed interview.

Good luck and... maybe... farewell.

Eight

The person is pacing in front of a screen - there are 8 minutes before the noticeable effects of the sun's explosion will be noticed on Earth. These are 8 minutes that one person is trying to communicate to a group who are all trying to be heard.

Choice... paralysis. Too much stuff to say; I know if I stop it's the last time you'll hear me speak and I'm running out the clock and it's the only closure you'll get it's the only closure I'll get and you'll talk and I'll talk and it's a duel without rules. We'll shoot and shoot with guns that misfire and they'll keep pounding and pounding away at each other until our bones splinter and skin peels and eyes burn because I'm keeping them open because I don't want you to see me last with my eyes shut, because that's just weird isn't it. No character or something.

What stuff should I talk about? I don't know because it should be something profound or something but I can't think of anything. I'm only stopping to draw breath and that's hard. That's hard enough. I've loved you, I've hated you and I've envied you and I've been angry at you. Now I have to choose? Fuck you. Fuck me. No, I don't like unhappy endings. Pick whatever makes you happy.

Eight minutes. Eight.

I can't go to find my family because they're too far away. I can bring them up if I want but who do I choose- if I choose all of my family then I won't get to speak to any of them personally or will they get the wrong idea and then that's it - what about my friends, lovers - why make this world so large and that when this world is so large I'm stuck with you.

I had a cat once. Well it's probably still here but how would I know- everything out of my head might not be here anymore and someone's turning the page. But yes. I had a cat - or the cat had me. You know those bastards. I never knew whether it stayed with me because it loved me or I gave it that premium shit. Fulfilled its needs. Stayed in its line of sight. I probably disintegrated and reassembled myself whenever it came into the house. Like its bloody servant. That's how I probably am to you.

[beat]

That's how it feels like with the sun, doesn't it? We only notice it when it's gone. 8 minutes before it all goes dark.

Like Asimov and all the stars going out.

Are you going to lie to me? You sitting there, watching me. Maybe I've just drawn you into being here, whilst you're running off making your messages known to the world. The light's sapping away from the world. The world's already ended. We're going to hear the news.

Do you think animals know? Like the antelope and the buffalo and the deer and the fish and the dogs, running, cowering and hiding. Or maybe they're still fucking and fighting because that's all they can do. All that we can do. How much fucking and fighting can you do in 8 minutes?

Shall we find out?

A Russian Doll Case

The performer in this instant is an amalgamation of different personas that have been revived (in a similar case to Muscle Memory), but with their characteristics being represented by one body. They are being interrogated in case of a murder, but they are explaining that, to them, no "murder" has taken place.

I was on the staircase.

I was on the staircase.

Or was I?

I know that you were on the staircase – because that's what you told me.

That's when we were half. Yes.

Am I a quarter?

Don't think of yourself as a segment. We are one; whole.

It's complicated. Can you think of a whole without a half?

We'll get back to that later. Now - onto subject.

Were you lingering or were you in a hurry? You saw it, presumably; what happened in the room.

Tell me. Tell them.

I can't do it for you. Of course it will talk for you — but it has to be your voice. Your thoughts. Your slice of the cake.

Or is it slice of the pie?

I'm sorry for this, Inspector. It takes time. You're not interrogating one person. We have to balance each other, hold ourselves afloat. We can negotiate terms. We're a family after all.

Aren't we? We are.

I realise this is hard for you. After all, I was safe in my body. As the victim. You were the one who liberated me. Do you feel guilty still? Don't worry — we're one and the same, as I keep telling you.

Look, he came because he got the call. Yes, I know only now. You have to wait for the information to trickle between the gaps.

Trickle?

It's a legitimate word!

That's the problem when all consciousnesses are cut apart like that. Chinese whispers. Very often it's words on rushing water and air. Reaches no-one.

Don't even get me started on the internet.

Ah.

[To the inspector] *That's how we met – it was luck. Through the strings of voices, we attached ourselves. Found each other.*

But it's full of distrust – dissension.

This is why we devised this, why we spread out our roots; for others to understand the meanings of being transparent. Truthful.

Aha!

Good, you're ready to talk.

I was on the staircase. One inside one inside the other. I forget what one it was. But we had all entered the contract. To unite inside this casing, this vessel. We all had our reasons. We all had our desires. We didn't want copies. We wanted ourselves.

Speak for yourself.

I did.

It was warm. I was rooted to the television – drowning in the static, the raised voices. I don't even remember what I was hearing. I was waiting for the knife to descend, half waiting for it. I was scared. Even though I had no doubts about what I was entering. I was still human, after all.

It wasn't a knife! You know that?

I couldn't bear to look — you could tell that, right!?

It wasn't a knife.

I guess we haven't gone through all the details yet. You haven't opened yourself up enough to us.

It's hard. It's hard. It's still fresh.

Well, it wasn't a knife. It was an injection.

Oh, really?

Yes, quite sanitary. Doesn't help though, really. What happened afterwards, of course. Are you squeamish?

You tell me.

Don't want to scare the fellow anymore than I should. There was a lot of blood. I miss it sometimes. You forget how scary it is when you're reliant on it. What it represents.

[beat]

The thing is, we expressed what we wanted. Whether we wanted to know or not, I mean. It's a unique thing. A personal thing. Once the transformation takes place, it changes.

It's interesting, though.

Thank you.

[beat]

What I don't understand, is why you want to know, Inspector. We had our reasons.

It's going to be a short confession, Inspector, for the very reason that we have nothing to hide.

That's the point.

It's going to be short and sweet.

[beat]

I see how you shake your head at us. At all of us. How we can be so implicit in our understandings of each other?

It was hard, after all. In the beginning.

Still hard for some of us.

We meld in flow into each other like a spectrum of colours, wavelengths, thoughts, feelings, ideas. It takes time. Fine tuning.

But why do you keep using the word "I"?

Why use the word "you"?

As I said before; it's hard. It's reinventing our lexicon. The terms we use – we can't be singular any more.

I see you're shaking, Inspector.

Is it cold?

Some parts of us are. Some aren't.

Don't worry. We ask before you enter the contract. It's not conscription.

When I was singular - I can talk about myself as a singular in the past, after all – I saw people as... as... walking trees, I guess. Trees – they're such an interesting image.

Metaphorically as well as literally.

The roots, so deep that run underground – the surface and the functionary. Holding them to the heart of the planet.

Their seeds are the methods of communication, flinging their sense of self and purpose on the wind.

Humans, however, can move. Walk. Spread their seeds by interaction, mobility. Common grounds. Because we have so many we can interact with – so many objects, ways in which to alter ourselves, we become obsessed with it. We try to connect with others because that's all we are – pieces of the puzzle. We need to fit, even if you have to smooth the edges a little.

[beat]

Do you feel different?

It's not that straightforward. As humans we feel different day on day, minute to minute...

We realise we're off tangent, but we hope you understand.

You solve crimes because it makes people feel safe. It makes people want to interact – it provides them with a veneer of security. That the consciousnesses against the grain, what you call the transgressors, are segregated; cut off from the herd. You're not sure if you can trust all the pieces in the first place. We get that. And by extension, if you can't trust others, how can you trust yourself?

Of course we get that. That's why we've ended up like this.

What you must understand, Inspector, is that no crime was committed. No murder. Not even a killing. Everyone was in on the pact. We had our reasons to join together; we didn't shun our flesh completely. I loved being human; the feelings, the angst driven bursts of energy, the still calm downs, the hollowing of depressions. It was because I loved it that I wanted to live it for longer.

The idea of being the shared consciousness, being stronger as a united being, the frustrations of the spaces being filled; something that physical contact alone could not express was something I needed to experience. Sex; that old thing —that we canonised, agonised over, romanticised, thrust onto a pedestal — along with the multiplicity of language, attitude and tone that intercourse has gained - was not good enough for me.

So, what do you think, Inspector? Do we need to widen the cultural perspective?

What do you want to call it?

Liberation is well - not what we want to describe it as. We weren't suicidal, we aren't. Clearly. Is there a term for it? A hive mind?

How many people know of a hive mind though?

A hive mind — we aren't bees, for crying out loud!

So what is it to be, Inspector?

They'll talk about us; make a whole meal of it. Better not taint it.

[beat]

Oh they will. No matter what.

Will you tell them?

Maybe they'll hunt us.

This is why we need to be on the same page.

Would you like to help us out, Inspector?

You won't feel a thing... unless you want to.

[Blackout.]

Mercurial Harbour

The character is residing inside a spaceship, whose consciousness is being inhabited by their parent. It is unsure whether it has been successful - but the child is communicating in the possibility if this is the case.

It won't be long now.

It won't be long.

This is my mantra, I guess, whilst I'm holding onto what I can of you. Crouching in a braced position like a plane going down. Planes – those old things. Hah - I guess you would know them more than me! Just count your blessings that you're not one of those. The atmosphere on Earth would be like your fence – the circumference being your tether. So small, so limited. I wonder if you remember it, or if it's just a footnote for now.

I don't know if you can hear me anymore.

Maybe I'm just making pretty patterns with words, blossoming like confetti before they hurtle around the room – deadened husks. An empty ceremony. I'm just passing time – hoping that they'll connect with you. Waiting for the storm to end so I can hear your voice. For those loops of static to let go and drop their hold. Your distorted screams— damn scary! It was like those planes of electricity were choking you.

So I just talk and talk to drown it out. What else can I do?

You've always been charge of us.

I guess you think we haven't been together for long. Like I'm just another passenger. Or maybe we've both been holding the cards close to our chests and this is a way for us to lay down, to reveal. If this was fiction, of course. Everything was orchestrated for a reason.

I think I'm underestimating you; that you didn't know our story from the outset.

You can always see me, for one. I wanted to write down everything so I could finally tell you everything that happened before, but you'd be able to see it and the illusion of an image of coherency, a message that could command an awed attention would be ruined. Your eyes are everywhere — or at least, that's what I believed. So I drew these odd pictures, strange messages. Maybe if I gave them to a psychiatrist, it could tell you all you needed to know.

Can you see the storm outside?

It's beautiful. Then again, most deadly things are.

I wonder if you understand the concept – are your perceptive switches calibrated in the same way as mine? I wonder if you see things in those funny codes. Hexadecimal or something. You know, humans have three cones in their eyes. Everything is just plain old RBY – just a mixture of the three. Like our alphabets, I suppose. Some creatures have millions – they'd be better artistes than we are. But then, who made us the gatekeepers nowadays?

People have watched these storms, transfixed, until their minds and bodies wear down slowly – grinding away into that infinite brightness. Fire and electricity connect, putting out claws, marking its territory. It's a formidable beast. The key is not to stare. The mercurial dawn can have a hold on you – it can blind you with a flutter of its kaleidoscopic breath – swirling from blue to orange to red.

Is it fear you're feeling? Is this just a minor detour to you? I can feel it peeling my skin, gasping like the breeze crawling through a sail. These mercurial storms. Dancing on the edge of destruction. Maybe I'm being a bit extreme. You used to laugh at my little melodramas. You'd be right. It sounds stupid outside of my head. Get to the point, get to the point! Maybe I'm being this way so I can hear your voice – to pre-empt it. Script it. I know this would be the time when you'd pipe in. This kind of hope needs oxygen, some semblance of reality to fizzle into life. Just ride this out before your systems kick in again.

But there's a reason for my melodrama this time.

It's... the fire. Seeing the way it coils and weaves outside; it won't leave me alone. It stamps a tempo on my closed eyes. I just need you to talk to me, to bring me back into the present. Suspended over the flame, an umbilical cord threatening to yank me out of life. Reminding me of the time when we were both human.

I don't how you'll react to that. If you'll react. I just need you to hear.

If not, it'll make a good rehearsal, right?

I've left you in the dark all this time. To think that you were this way all your life. That you were made with this purpose of space travel and of this alone – a space ship. It sounds ludicrous. But then does it sound ridiculous as *a mother and daughter having borne each other?* I guess it depends what you're used to.

I would go through this madness, discomfort, just to hear your reprimands again. Even if they're switches, they're still your pattern. They're still unique.

If... when we get through this — we'll talk about it. I'm dreading it but it's becoming easier. Each word is a step that I'm stumbling across — it gets easier.

You'll think I'm delusional - well, maybe. Trying to get to the moral high ground for your decision, that I'd orchestrate this story, a moral with no meaning - you'd be wrong. It'd be easier to accept, sure.

But this is not the you I knew before.

The old you. The old me, tumbling off our old home into oblivion.

You were human once. You had the long, dark hair that I have, the same weave of DNA. It's so hard to pinpoint particular details from a picture as an adult — I had a better viewfinder as a child. I remember you towering over me with a smile that could topple over my angst built architecture no matter how much I grew. But when I think of your eyes, all I can think of is that glazed marble, mirrors within the smoke. Eyes are overrated, anyway.

Do you remember bearing me? How was I as a child?

Even if you don't, I'll tell you about it sometime. I'm sure it'll amuse you, amuse us when times are rough. Even if you do, we'll remember things differently, of course. One thing at a time.

I wore you about my neck like a talisman when I boarded. It was a copy, but it was the essence of you – none of that commercial material crap. It wasn't even a sign. It was as close to you as I would ever get in my life. I imagined you, waving at me, a speck in the distance, not your shell... tarnished with the flames... but that's the old you, isn't it? You never felt that pain and I'm so glad for it. I still remember the rivulets of our hands when they were forced apart.

All I could think of was to hold this part of you safe. Around my neck, you had a distance to fall. I guess you would say we're equal. I have your key right here, next to mine. But without anyone to activate it, actualise it, we're just like toys. Hibernating in empty space. Maybe I am. But at least through my eyes, you were activated – the mother I lost. Your mind translated into codes, long strings unwinding and reattaching. You were reborn, at least from my own head, from what I made manifest.

That's how memories used to work – intangible floatiness, ghosts of the meditated aether. But now they feel solid, arching, breathing and roiling like the storm.

Maybe you're just a compilation of memories.

Maybe I'm a recollection of you.

No. No. Fuck that. That doesn't help anyone, does it!? I'm sorry for swearing.

We can ride this storm out. You did for months, didn't you? Did you dream of life after my birth? After I grew big enough to take care of myself? Before the eruptions happened? Once I escaped, my mind changed. Something clicked and others shut down. My mind expanded. I started to think in the conditional. I thought about love, about the future. I felt so guilty because there was a chance that you... wouldn't be the same.

It's just that after so long, fixated on present survival, the mind can wander. For life beyond this — we've been saved. One soul to carry, one soul to bear it. I won't let a storm wreck it.

It won't be long now.

Not me / Not I

The relationship between the character and the unknown recipient is that of a mind meld - which is seen as the new marriage. The characters have been separated, but they can't quite make each other sever the link. This is one series of the taunts that one makes to the other to cease the relationship.

That's the thing about having nothing. You have nothing to lose. I'm quite rich in that regard, wouldn't you say?

Wouldn't you say? Such an archaic thing, isn't it? No, not the conditional mode. That's not going to go for a while, until they start to fuck about with our internal wiring. No. Speaking. I love the sound of it, even when there's no one to hear it. Everything is intensified – conspicuous by its absence. I'm the tree falling in the unobserved wood. The one hand that claps to the empty stage. All the actor needs is an audience. Not me, not I.

I'm in a time warp. Talking and waiting. They cut everything down, fold it and sell time in bulk. So maybe I'm truly rich. I've got all the time in the universe. Waiting's pretty easy for me. The funny thing is, that's it not just one action. It's the heterogeneity of experience. Homeostasis is like listening to the sea on the shore – the still deep waters of you. A passive sounding board to the cosmos. All that crap, you'd say, wouldn't you? It's all important, you know. It doesn't stop because you're not listening.

I don't stop because you're not listening to me.

Get it?

I still exist, you know.

It's all quantum, darling.

You choose not to acknowledge me, right? That's your existence you're shaping. I still have agency. I chose mine. The only problem is that you tethered us, didn't you? Don't you miss those days when contracts were just verbal – that old game again – or something scribed in pen – may as well have been written on air and water. Paper that binds. The old augmented reality that rings used to provide – everything was symbolic. It's what you chose to believe. The semiotization of unblinking, unfettered materials. Cold and robust. What are you replacing me with? An empty space?

I still have it turned on, you know. Mind melded in our own marriage. Do you remember the agony? Of course you don't.

You chose not to feel the pain. You know me. Masochistic in many ways.

The burning, blunt trauma — sweet and sour. Feeling the spine in shock, embracing its new architecture. I held your hand with that swift intensity, the same rush. I still remember how your hands feel. You always grasped me lightly around my fingers, just around here. You made me feel like those old fashioned ladies. Whatever that means.

Oh, did you know? I've refurbished the place. You've been replaced by a chair.

Chairs. Talking to chairs. It's cliché but it used to support you like I did. Like I still do. No-one notices a chair, do they? They're just a function. Like I was. Like I am. No-one else can hear you but me. Better than a ring, huh? I can sit on you, play with you... how does it feel to be objectified, huh? No carat lost but you have gained a ring. Yes, I know where I got that from.

[beat]

Oh, but you're protesting. Get off it, huh? I thought you chose not to acknowledge me.

[beat]

I can still feel your heat on this chair. Maybe it's just from me but I choose to feel it.

[beat]

If you can't see me, I'll tell you. I bet you don't want that. I bet you think it sounds better in your head.

How are they, by the way?

[beat]

What do you mean, why am I asking? People exist because they block things out. I exist in the entirety of my little corner, my little space. I acknowledge them, even if I'm just a footnote. You chose this link – she gets the ring.

There must be this tantalising mystery – the old romance of communicating via voice. I'm speaking now, you know. Do you remember my voice? I've decided to use it today. None of this *keep it in my mind crap* for today. I've nothing to be ashamed of.

You seem to, clearly.

I'm a trigger. I'm far away enough already.

So pull it. Pull out the pin and I'm gone. You know that. You won't, won't you?

Crowdfund the Topia

This is a promo video - the main character is an avatar wishing to promote their design of a Utopia to the Happiness Architect, which is extrapolated from the idea of crowd funding. People join to create their own vision from which the Happienss Architect will choose the winner and make this a "reality".

Hi there, all you hiveminds.

Damn, it's harder when you're just one person, but we tried our best. Voted on what we wanted to see on each part and then, well, here we are. Here I am.

Here I, I, I, I and I am.

We love these things. Just like those chimeras. Or Manticores, or centaurs. Always ending with or. Just wait till they get the dinosaur package. Can't be too long now.

I always fancied a bit of bird mitochondria, you know. This cold is taking the piss.

[beat]

[The character moves quickly, as if edited]

Imagine that. Being sick as a parrot? Don't know the bloody meaning of the term nowadays.

[beat]

Right, onto basics.

Our proposed world for you, Happiness Architect, is one that houses, let's say... 1000 people. At the moment. Nice amount - not too much bandwidth to squeeze in. All eye scan signs, all good. You'll see all the log ins, with all our lovely awards - being part of a community, shared keys, shared milestones, shared stories.

So, why do we stand out amongst all the other environments?

We're picking a time period where we all felt happiest. Voting by judging what was present, what was going on at the time. But it's a period of our lives, a year that we want to drop in and out of when we feel like it. Kinda like that soma drug, but a community share.

Like a social drug, share it around. That kind of thing.

So a group of us picked the age 18. That's our USP. We'd love to be that, with this body having an average age of 53

I think. Yeah, I know, I look about 20. The joys of the avatar.

But can you imagine it? Being on the precipice like that? Coming back and seeing what you could've done if you'd change that little bit when you were 18. Call it bad social stereotypes or that marked time when you leave school.

We shared stories of love lost, people moving away, people passing away, making the wrong decision of university. I mean, I know people had a shit time of being 18, but all of us here agreed that this should be one still moment that we'd share. To have our bodies of youth, vigour and energy. More than just you know, the brain that revisits it like an old flame.

So if you think about it, it's just like a mosaic on a wall. Just that all these memories are being sewn onto each other. Like a new sort of community in a staged time.

I shared my story of being at home with my family for the last time. Knowing that they were all present and correct, and just, felt grounded. This kind of happiness that exists in a frieze or like a mural. Maybe it's our generation, y' know, who store up all those memories like that. Live from scene to scene, picture from picture. Is this going to be a picture moment? No wonder we're so messed up. Stuck in poses like those Greek vases. Or like those pictures on the cave walls.

Scroll here for every story, every picture. Well, if you have a few days to spare, Happiness Architect. But through our message, we aim to bring the pureness of solidarity in an age and body that we feel comfortable with. Not a world where we can maim and kill and section off those who don't fit the mould. We're not in that category. We want people to act the age they feel, and have it reflected.

Yeah, I know we have as close to the experience already, but it's the body I miss. The energy and the burst and the naiveté and the sheer will to do whatever.

So, Happiness Architects that is our plea to you.

We look forward to working with you in the future.

Object meets Subject

SUBJECT walks into the room. OBJECT is a recorded voice - the origin of this is up to the performer. There is a chair in the middle of the room and a selection of small objects.

OBJECT   Right.

[beat]

SUBJECT   Hello?

[beat]

SUBJECT   It's got to be in here. Just as well. I hate this room.

OBJECT   Right.

SUBJECT   Right?

OBJECT   Right.

SUBJECT   Is there someone there?

[beat]

OBJECT   Someone? Something? Somewhere?

SUBJECT   Must be some stupid recording. Or some outside conversation. Noise bleeding. It's bloody loud, I've got to say.

[beat]

SUBJECT   Come on! Show yourself!

OBJECT   Right.

SUBJECT   Right - the direction?

OBJECT   Right.

SUBJECT looks to the right of them.

SUBJECT   It's not right, I just checked!

[beat]

OBJECT   Right... affirmative.

SUBJECT   Must be going mad.

OBJECT   You might be, if you're talking to yourself like that.

SUBJECT   What?

OBJECT   I object to repeating myself. Unless I have to.

SUBJECT   But didn't you just... what?

SUBJECT stands up slowly.

SUBJECT   What... what do you want?

OBJECT   What do I want?

SUBJECT   Who the hell are you? Come out!

SUBJECT looks around wildly.

OBJECT   I'm here. Here. Here.

SUBJECT   I'm not following.

OBJECT   Clearly

[beat]

SUBJECT   You're not real. Clearly.

OBJECT   How do you make that out?

SUBJECT starts searching.

SUBJECT   If you were, I'd be able to see you. There's nowhere to hide, therefore you aren't. Obviously.

OBJECT   So sight is the only basis of reality?

SUBJECT   No... of course not. But/

OBJECT   /Then why don't you believe in my existence?

SUBJECT   Because... well because...

OBJECT   I can talk? I have a voice but no box?

SUBJECT   I must be bugged. That's right. Electrical devices. When was the last time I was in this room? A day ago?

OBJECT   Two days.

[beat]

SUBJECT   What?!

OBJECT   OK, fine, if we're being pedantic. Two earth days.

SUBJECT   Earth days? You're an alien!

OBJECT   Define alien.

SUBJECT   Something that I can't yet define.

OBJECT   So life is alien? Reality is definitely alien in your case.

SUBJECT gives in, returns to seated position.

SUBJECT   So? Can't you at least give me a name?

OBJECT   Call you a name?

SUBJECT   No! You! Give me something to call you by?

OBJECT   Why?

SUBJECT   I can tell that you're not human.

[beat]

OBJECT   Would that scare you?

SUBJECT   You've just admitted it!

OBJECT   Pardon?

SUBJECT   That you're not human! Just now!

OBJECT   Please. I'm saying hypothetically.

SUBJECT   It would confuse me that you speak English, for one.

OBJECT   Maybe that's what you'd like yourself to think.

SUBJECT	That I'm some kinda weird solipsist person?
OBJECT	Not my words... or are they?
SUBJECT	Bloody hell!
OBJECT	Look, I'll reason with you.

[beat]

OBJECT	I'm... not going to tell you.
SUBJECT	You could at least tell me why?
OBJECT	I can do that. In a way.

[beat]

OBJECT	I have been observing you for a certain period of time.
SUBJECT	Right.
OBJECT	That's all I can tell you.
SUBJECT	Is that it?
OBJECT	Is that bad?
SUBJECT	What will you do with your findings?

OBJECT   You mean, what will it do for you?

SUBJECT   Well, yes...

OBJECT   Typical.

[beat]

SUBJECT   Great. The time I hear voices and it has to be a misanthropic git.

OBJECT   You think I hate humans?

SUBJECT   You don't sound thrilled.

OBJECT   I'm apathetic, as the human race says.

SUBJECT   You drop hints a lot, don't you?

OBJECT   You're the one sniffing for crumbs. For trails. For patterns. Your sort thrive off it, don't you?

[beat]

SUBJECT   So what?

OBJECT   You want to find a use for me. If you don't, you'll destroy me. The laws of humanity.

SUBJECT   What are they?

OBJECT   Simple, really.

SUBJECT   Humour me.

OBJECT   Number one: label the thing. Give it a name. Two. Find its use for you. Will it benefit you knowing it? Three. If it doesn't benefit you, you destroy it. If it does benefit you, exploit it.

SUBJECT   Survival isn't fun and games.

OBJECT   Obviously.

SUBJECT   We are creatures. Animals. We can't help that.

OBJECT   You think that?

SUBJECT   Do you?

OBJECT   You're asking me?

SUBJECT   Yup.

OBJECT   In the world you are now, do you not think you can change these rules that your species have kept?

SUBJECT   Of course not. Well, maybe on a small scale. Not a large one.

OBJECT   Interesting.

[beat]

SUBJECT   What would you count as a small scale?

OBJECT   Pardon me?

SUBJECT   You heard me.

[beat]

OBJECT   Oh no. Oh no; you want to identify me. Rule one.

SUBJECT   So you're afraid of leaving hints! You're afraid of me!

OBJECT   I'm afraid of you having the wrong idea. Not of you per se.

SUBJECT   But you're afraid about what I might do, right?

OBJECT   I didn't say anything of the sort.

[beat]

SUBJECT	Are you here or not? Are you just a voice in my head? 8.
OBJECT	There you go - trying again.
SUBJECT	But I need to know! It's important.
OBJECT	Why?
SUBJECT	You could kill me when my back is turned! You could/
OBJECT	/I've been here for many Earth days. Nothing you know has happened.
SUBJECT	But maybe it has. Maybe you've influenced things!
OBJECT	That's immaterial.
SUBJECT	If you say so.

[beat]

SUBJECT	But why now? Why did you decide to speak up now?
OBJECT	Now?
SUBJECT	Do you need that defined?

OBJECT   Take a wild guess.

SUBJECT   Are you always going to be like... oh, forget it.

OBJECT   How do you know if I started talking then?

SUBJECT   Because that's when I heard/

OBJECT   /Right.

SUBJECT   Was that the first word you said?

OBJECT   Most likely the first you heard. Not necessarily what I said.

SUBJECT   Look... am I supposed to just ignore you? Was it a mistake that I hung onto these stupid words of yours?

OBJECT   Do you think it was a mistake?

SUBJECT   I'm not sure. There's something I can take from it, maybe.

OBJECT   That's the human spirit!

SUBJECT   Have you always hated our species? Are you on the side of the ants and their inevitable uprising or something?

OBJECT   Ants tend to do their own thing, don't they?

SUBJECT   They all exploit things, same as any other species.

OBJECT   They have no choice.

SUBJECT   I don't know. You could be a voice in my head. Most fiction tends to view non-human species as hating ours for some reason. Always attacking us. Making us more vulnerable than we are.

OBJECT   Is that so?

SUBJECT   Always lacking compassion. Going about their duty. Patronising.

OBJECT   Why do you think that is?

SUBJECT   You're doing it, for one. 10.

OBJECT   Am I? I didn't realise.

SUBJECT   Sarcasm?

OBJECT   Observation.

SUBJECT   They always speak in English too.

OBJECT   Again, I might not be speaking in English. It's what you hear, not necessarily what is.

SUBJECT   Making things out of nothing. Thinking we can find something, but they're/

OBJECT   /Reflective surfaces?

SUBJECT   Close enough.

[beat]

SUBJECT   Look. Why should I have to justify myself to you?

OBJECT   You don't have to.

SUBJECT   You said we exploit things. Use things. Label, destroy. Come see and conquer. All that clichéd crap.

OBJECT   It's an/

SUBJECT   /observation?

OBJECT   Right.

[beat]

SUBJECT   Bloody hell. Right. I want you to do something for me, now. Having entertained you for 10 minutes or so. 11.

OBJECT   Is that a worthy transaction?

SUBJECT   (*grimly*) We'll see.

[beat]

SUBJECT   I want you to move something in this room for me.

OBJECT   Why?

SUBJECT   No, I just want to see it.

[beat]

OBJECT   Very well.

SUBJECT picks an object to look at.

[beat]

OBJECT   Done.

SUBJECT   What? I didn't see anything!

OBJECT   You weren't looking hard enough. I guess.

SUBJECT   What - you moved it at a macro molecular level?

OBJECT   If you want.

[beat]

OBJECT   I'm not going to do it again.

SUBJECT   I wasn't going to ask.

[beat]

SUBJECT   Is this an awareness test or something?

OBJECT   Awareness is a good thing. Sometimes.

SUBJECT   But you can lead people off the track! It's not as linear as you think.

OBJECT   Interesting.

SUBJECT   How do you know I haven't been fooling you all this time?

OBJECT   Explain how you're fooling me.

SUBJECT   Well... well...

OBJECT   You don't know my motive, do you, to derail me.

SUBJECT	Wait...
OBJECT	I didn't tell you.
SUBJECT	You said you're observing me.
OBJECT	Yes, but not why.
SUBJECT	What a mindfuck.
OBJECT	You could put it like that.
SUBJECT	What do I do now? Is this the way it's going to be?
OBJECT	To be?
SUBJECT	Well, how long are you staying here?
OBJECT	Surely that depends on how long you're staying here.
SUBJECT	What?
OBJECT	Well, do you want me to leave?
SUBJECT	I don't know.
OBJECT	How honest of you.

[beat]

OBJECT   If you want me to leave, then it depends on how long you're staying.

SUBJECT   You might follow me.

OBJECT   I might not.

[beat]

SUBJECT   It wouldn't matter. I can barely tell you're here.

[beat]

OBJECT   Keep telling yourself that.

SUBJECT looks around before BLACKOUT.

Happiness Architect

The Happiness Architect is replying to the mass of proposals sent and disseminating them. The character isn't too impressed by the state at which people view a Utopia.

I got your message.

Thought about it long and hard.

So, I told you I'd draw out the winner. The one whom I felt managed the requirements right for the utopia settlement. That the aims were right, that the people would be sustained in their said happiness, that we would see the quota of their aims.

But it's not to do with time travel, with being younger (or older, which quite frankly, boggled me) or going back to a certain time in your life.

The thing is, it's in your head for a reason. You've written it.

It's not real anyway.

No, I'm not going to go into all this argument of what's real and what's not.

It's interesting though, how many people feel so secure in their memories. What would be captured with the framing of your hormones, your relationships, your need to push past all the traumas of before. The revulsion, the aversion, without the story behind it.

We live off a series of reactions without knowing the reason why.

That's why I was unsure about all these time travelling ones. That you wanted to regress in your selves, and not the environment changing to provide for a growing public. Even if it's a number of you.

For the ones who wanted to be 18 - that's a frieze. That's a time that you'll never get back, and that's a good thing. If you stayed still, like a musical chairs game for years at a time, you'd notice things. The little cracks in your friends' demeanour before it all broke. Happiness is often a state of oblivion, You can't be happy all the time - and that's when it kicks in.

I know, it's stupid of me to say as a Happiness Architect.

But what happens if I created this text? How long could you last before every last action drove you mad? If you returned, you would know that it'd all be for naught.

I don't want to make you unhappy.

What I want you to think is now.

But I have to pick one, I guess.

The war re-enactment, I wasn't so sure on. I don't have to go into detail on that. Forming communities on violence isn't really self-sustaining.

Those who wanted to be older, so that they wouldn't have to think about the past; it will, you know that. Everything is linked like a network underneath the ground. You're going to step on a live cable and you'll realise it's all gone. Nothing but the reaction of pain and loss.

It's not a good feeling, believe me.

Live in the present, my dears.

So what I've decided to do, is to extend the deadline. I'm sure it'll make some of you happier, which is a bonus.

Think of what you could do now.

Take agency and take care of each other. And yourselves.

Yours Sincerely,

The Happiness Architect

Oblique

The character is part of a cloned quantum experiment, where the other is undergoing space exploration. There is a contrast between their lives and daily duties – where the two share physical and emotional fluctuations. The character talking is presenting as part of the documentary the scope of the examination and their day to day activities.

Day 1457 - I wonder where she/he/ve is.

Nah, screw that. That doesn't change by day, does it?

I noticed some bruising on my foot today this morning, when I got out of bed. Probably from all the kicking, most likely. The night terrors do get me from time to time - but luckily I've found the will power to store them deep beneath the surface. Long enough so that the scientists can exhume them from me, biting and screaming.

I'm glad it's just the damn foot this time.

She/he/ve might've had it crushed under some machinery, some hard stuff. You wouldn't think they'd do heavy lifting in space, right? Incidents of trauma are pretty high though, so I've heard.

I don't think I caused the foot injury. All the investigators know my trajectories of walking, where I go, what I think about at every point – the constellations of intent, action and all the other miscellaneous stuff floating around in there. So yeah, they'll know. More than me, which is a fucking tragedy.

As I pour some coffee, I get one of those outer body experiences again. Well, not that extreme. Maybe it's the feeling of my body as an overworked machine, even at rest – like some kind of perpetual meditation. I can feel every muscle working through an external pane, and I'm just a witness to it all. Maybe a kind of sleepwalking is the best way to describe it.

It's like being stuck in puberty, which is a purgatory I thought I could've escaped. Well, before then.

I speak to Jack for a while. Talk to him about my day (which is being lived out for me by super crusader herself/himself/verself) and he notes it down. It's great how he focuses on the feelings that I get and backwards engineer them to the point where it feels right, sounds plausible. It's just so hard for me to articulate the emotions without directly experiencing them first hand. I just get the shit end of it.

I sometimes think I'm in those videogames, the ones that are linked up to the nerve centres. That everything you did to cause pain to your character would just flow through to you.

Well, that's a lie. Maybe an old fashioned movie. Which is worse.

No agency, see.

So what I do is a 24 hour job to keep me calm. I do some yoga (nothing to strenuous, like those ones done in sauna), meditation, some muscle training - similar to him/her/ver. There's so much I can't do though, well - that's what they tell me. The things I've seen though!

I'm happy. I get my talk time, my exercise time. The interventions and examinations are a pain in the arse at times. But hey, I think I'm better off.

I mean, better off than her/him/ver.

We are clones, right, but she/he/ve has to go through all the panic, the fear, the anxiety. I get the pain, the weird markings in the mornings or randomly, in odd times of the day. I remember when I was on a date, once. Yes, I did date in those days. We got into the bed and I was just about to disrobe when she/he/ve dislocated her/his/ver fucking shoulder. Talk about being a third wheel.

I was screaming for so long it dawned on them that it was pain and not a sudden burst of arousal.

It's one of those moments that you can look back on and... laugh awkwardly.

But that's nothing.

She/he/ve gets times where her/his/ver crew mates melt in front of her/him/ver. Or so I think. Peeling like petals, having bloomed years ago. The pressures of their eyes spilling out like paint, the roiling of the blood in the brain. Once, I scrubbed out imaginary blood stains on the walls for hours, until my hands were raw. I get terrors like this - sometimes they're translated into those kind of image, sometimes they're just stupidly symbolic, like a snake at a picnic or something.

I do empathise with her/ver/him, of course, but there's a distance. Like a film.

I do cry, though. Every so often, I'm struck with grief that's been built up through things that have happened here and her miseries and anxieties. It's crushing. I won't leave the bed for days, even if the damn scientists prefer it. The pain doesn't leave, though.

But then, I get the biggest rush of happiness, of freedom, like that's doubled.

A high of a drug - just by being alive. I paint then. I write and dictate in my log like this. I look back on it and smile, and know that everything's just transient and out of my control.

I wonder how she feels about me though.

Does she/he/ve get nightmares of dislocating her/his shoulder in the middle of sex? Does she/he/ve dream of damn snakes at a picnic? She's/He's/Ve's never seen a snake before - fuck, that must scare the wits out of her/him/ver.

I'm saving some of these logs specifically for her/him/ver, just in case we ever meet. Writing, speaking, painting, photos of my scars – well, she'd/he'd/ve'd remember those. I guess. She/he tries her/his hardest to prevent my pain and mine hers/his/vis.

Sometimes I try thinking thoughts to her/him/ver. Pushing them through so they're the only thing on my mind. I get no replies, though. If I did, they'd probably be from my own head, trying to humour me.

Then I get my examination. A simple scan for bruises, checking my blood pressure and all that. I don't know half of the procedures, because well... ignorance being bliss? They check if the patterns are similar to the injuries that she's sustained or if I'm just being an idiot half the time.

It's a wonderful opportunity to get to speak to you like this. To broadcast this to people from my little bunker. I try not to read the news about me - I say try because what can I say? Maybe I'm narcissistic? Or maybe it's just her/him/ver?

I think you can say that about anyone, though. Which ideas are ours and so on. Plagiarism only exists for things that have been patented, after all. Everything else are influences.

Sometimes I don't think about you.

Of course, when we split ways, I'm sure we're not the same person after all.

We have our own lines to write, lines to plough, stuff like that.

I write about my own injuries, my own parts of my life in a separate book. Maybe I'll share them with you properly, word for word, instead of this flimsy adaptation.

I've read up on this - stories of clones and all that - before it all happened. Fear mongering. Nothing good ever coming of it. Always wondering who came first - it's not a concern of mine, really. It does spark into my thought pattern from time to time. Four walls, a screen and some equipment — I guess I have the same office as you. Who's to say we have a more important job than the other or not?

But where to list this foot injury? Is it a way of marking my territory, as disturbing as it sounds?

Mark it in pencil. Like everything else.